Starting a Dump Truck Business

Do You Want to Know the Breakthrough Strategies for Dominating the Dump Truck Industry?

Content

Chapter 1.   Introduction

Starting a dump truck business can be a lucrative and rewarding venture, but it also requires careful planning and preparation. Whether you're an experienced entrepreneur or new to the business world, this guide will help you navigate the process of starting and growing a successful dump truck business.

The dump truck business is a vital component of the construction and mining industries, as well as many other industries that require the transportation of materials from one place to another. Dump trucks are used to haul everything from dirt and gravel to sand, rocks, and other heavy materials, making them a critical tool for many businesses.

As a business owner, you'll need to consider a wide range of factors when starting your dump truck business. From securing financing and choosing the right equipment, to building a strong network of customers and developing a marketing strategy, there are many things to consider. Additionally, you'll need to be familiar with the legal and regulatory requirements of operating a dump truck business, as well as the various industry trends and technological advances that are impacting the sector.

In this guide, we'll walk you through the process of starting a dump truck business, step by step. We'll cover everything from developing a business plan and conducting a feasibility study, to managing your fleet, building a strong customer base, and preparing for the future of the business. We'll also explore the key challenges that you'll face as a dump truck business owner, and provide practical advice and strategies for overcoming them.

Whether you're just starting out or looking to take your dump truck business to the next level, this guide is designed to provide you with the information and insights you need to succeed. So, let's get started!

Chapter 2.   Understanding the Market and Competition

Before starting your dump truck business, it's important to understand the market and competition you'll be entering. Understanding your competition will help you identify opportunities, avoid potential pitfalls, and develop a strong strategy for success.

Market research is the key to understanding the market and competition for your dump truck business. Start by analyzing the demand for dump truck services in your area. Look at the types of construction and mining projects that are taking place, as well as the industries that rely on the transportation of heavy materials. This information will help you determine the potential demand for your services and identify any potential gaps in the market that you can fill.

Next, research your competition. Look at the types of dump truck businesses operating in your area and what they offer. Take note of their pricing strategies, customer service offerings, and marketing tactics. This information will help you identify opportunities to differentiate yourself from your competition and provide better value to your customers.

Once you've conducted your market research, you'll be in a much better position to develop a strong strategy for success. Use your research to identify your target market and create a unique value proposition that sets you apart from your competition. This could include offering superior customer service, providing specialized services, or utilizing innovative technologies to streamline your operations.

It's also important to stay up-to-date with industry trends and technological advances that are impacting the dump truck business. Attend trade shows and conferences, read industry publications, and connect with other business owners to stay informed about the latest developments.

In conclusion, understanding the market and competition is a critical step in starting a successful dump truck business. By conducting thorough market research and staying informed about industry trends and developments, you'll be in a strong position to develop a competitive strategy and grow your business.

Chapter 3.   Developing a Business Plan

A business plan is a comprehensive roadmap for your dump truck business. It outlines your goals and objectives, as well as the strategies and actions you'll take to achieve them. A well-written business plan is also an essential tool for securing financing, attracting investors, and establishing a strong foundation for your business.

When developing your business plan, it's important to be as detailed and comprehensive as possible. Start by outlining your business concept, including the services you'll offer, your target market, and your unique value proposition. This will serve as the foundation for your plan and help you clarify your vision for your business.

Next, research and analyze your market, competition, and industry trends. This information will help you develop realistic projections for sales and profits, as well as identify potential challenges and opportunities. Be sure to include a detailed marketing and sales strategy, as well as a thorough operational plan that outlines how you'll manage your fleet and run your business day-to-day.

It's also important to include a financial plan that outlines your projected expenses, revenue, and profits. This will help you determine the capital you'll need to start and grow your business, as well as assess the viability of your business concept. Be sure to include detailed budgets for equipment, personnel, and marketing, as well as a break-even analysis that will help you determine when your business will start to generate a profit.

Finally, make sure to review your business plan regularly and make changes as needed. This will help you stay on track and adapt to changes in the market, competition, or industry.

In conclusion, a business plan is an essential tool for starting and growing a successful dump truck business. By taking the time to research, analyze, and outline your business concept, you'll have a comprehensive roadmap to follow as you launch and grow your business.

Chapter 4.   Conducting a Feasibility Study

Before starting your dump truck business, it's important to conduct a feasibility study to determine whether your business concept is viable and to identify any potential challenges. A feasibility study is an in-depth analysis of your business idea, including the market, competition, and industry trends.

To start, research and analyze the demand for dump truck services in your area. Look at the types of construction and mining projects that are taking place, as well as the industries that rely on the transportation of heavy materials. This information will help you determine the potential demand for your services and identify any potential gaps in the market that you can fill.

Next, research and analyze your competition. Look at the types of dump truck businesses operating in your area and what they offer. Take note of their pricing strategies, customer service offerings, and marketing tactics. This information will help you identify opportunities to differentiate yourself from your competition and provide better value to your customers.

It's also important to assess the costs and expenses associated with starting and operating a dump truck business. This will include costs for equipment, personnel, fuel, insurance, and maintenance, as well as any ongoing operational expenses. You'll also need to factor in the cost of obtaining the necessary licenses and permits to operate your business.

In addition to conducting a financial analysis, it's also important to assess the regulatory environment for dump truck businesses in your area. This will include researching the laws and regulations that apply to the transportation of heavy materials, as well as the requirements for obtaining the necessary licenses and permits.

Finally, use the information you've gathered to determine the viability of your business concept. Consider whether there is enough demand for your services, whether you have a competitive advantage, and whether the costs and expenses associated with starting and operating your business are manageable.

In conclusion, conducting a feasibility study is a critical step in starting a successful dump truck business. By researching and analyzing the market, competition, and industry trends, you'll be in a much better position to determine whether your business idea is viable and to identify any potential challenges.

Chapter 5.   Building a Strong Network

Building a strong network of contacts is an important aspect of starting and growing a successful dump truck business. A well-established network can provide valuable resources, support, and opportunities for your business, as well as help you overcome obstacles and reach your goals.

One of the first steps in building a strong network is to identify the key players in your industry. This may include suppliers, contractors, and other businesses that offer complementary services to yours. Reach out to these companies and introduce yourself, share your business concept, and explain how you can work together to serve your mutual customers.

It's also important to join trade associations and organizations related to the transportation and construction industries. These organizations provide valuable networking opportunities, as well as access to industry information, training programs, and business resources.

In addition to building a network of professional contacts, it's also important to develop strong relationships with your customers. Provide excellent customer service and be responsive to their needs. Consider offering loyalty programs and other incentives to keep your customers coming back.

Another way to build a strong network is to engage with your community. Consider participating in local events, supporting local charities, and offering your services to local organizations. This will help you establish your business as a valuable and trustworthy member of the community, and may lead to new business opportunities.

Finally, make sure to leverage your personal and professional networks as well. Reach out to family, friends, and former colleagues, and let them know about your new business. They may be able to offer support, introduce you to potential customers, or provide other resources that can help you grow your business.

In conclusion, building a strong network is an important aspect of starting and growing a successful dump truck business. By establishing relationships with key players in your industry, engaging with your community, and leveraging your personal and professional networks, you'll be well-positioned to overcome obstacles and reach your goals.

Chapter 6.   Legal and Regulatory Requirements

Starting a dump truck business involves navigating a complex web of legal and regulatory requirements. Failure to comply with these requirements can result in significant fines, penalties, and even legal action, so it's important to understand what's required of your business from the outset.

One of the first steps in starting your business is to obtain the necessary licenses and permits. This will vary depending on the location of your business, but may include a commercial driver's license, a DOT number, and permits for operating heavy equipment. In addition, you may also need to obtain business licenses, insurance, and bonding.

It's also important to understand the regulations that apply to the transportation of heavy materials. This may include regulations regarding the size and weight of the load, as well as requirements for securement and inspection of the load. Familiarize yourself with these regulations and ensure that your business is in compliance with them.

Another important consideration is the employment laws and regulations that apply to your business. This will include minimum wage requirements, overtime laws, and worker's compensation requirements. In addition, you may also need to provide your employees with proper training and certification, as well as maintain a safe work environment.

In addition to the legal and regulatory requirements specific to your business, you'll also need to comply with general business laws and regulations. This will include accounting and tax requirements, as well as requirements for record-keeping, reporting, and documentation.

Finally, it's important to understand the insurance requirements for your business. This will include liability insurance, which protects your business in the event of an accident, as well as workers' compensation insurance, which provides coverage for your employees in the event of injury or illness.

In conclusion, navigating the legal and regulatory requirements of starting a dump truck business can be a complex and challenging process. However, by familiarizing yourself with the requirements specific to your business, and working with a knowledgeable attorney or regulatory agency, you'll be well-positioned to ensure that your business is in compliance with all applicable laws and regulations.

Chapter 7.   Securing Financing

Securing financing is a critical component of starting a successful dump truck business. Depending on the size of your business and the amount of capital you require, there are a number of different financing options available.

One of the first steps in securing financing is to create a detailed business plan. This plan should outline your business concept, market opportunity, and financial projections. In addition, it should also detail how you plan to use the financing you secure and how you will repay the loan or investment.

Once you have a solid business plan in place, you can start exploring financing options. If you have personal savings or investments, you may consider using these funds to start your business. Alternatively, you may be able to secure a small business loan from a traditional lender, such as a bank or credit union.

In addition to traditional lending options, there are also a number of alternative financing options available, including crowdfunding, peer-to-peer lending, and angel investment. These options can provide flexible and creative financing solutions for businesses that may not meet the requirements of traditional lenders.

Another financing option to consider is government-sponsored financing, such as grants and loans from the Small Business Administration (SBA). These programs can provide valuable financing options for small businesses, as well as support and resources to help you grow your business.

In conclusion, securing financing is a critical component of starting a successful dump truck business. By creating a detailed business plan, exploring financing options, and working with a knowledgeable financial advisor, you'll be well-positioned to secure the funding you need to grow your business and reach your goals.

Chapter 8.   Choosing the Right Truck and Equipment

Choosing the right truck and equipment is a critical component of starting a successful dump truck business. The right equipment can help you get the job done efficiently and effectively, while the wrong equipment can result in increased costs and decreased productivity.

The first step in choosing the right truck and equipment is to assess your business needs. Consider the type of work you'll be doing, the materials you'll be transporting, and the environment in which you'll be working. Based on this information, you can determine the size and capacity of the truck you'll need, as well as the type of dump body and other equipment you'll require.

Once you've assessed your needs, it's important to consider your budget. Dump trucks and equipment can be expensive, so it's important to carefully evaluate your financial resources and determine how much you can afford to spend.

Another important factor to consider when choosing equipment is reliability and durability. Make sure to choose equipment that is well-built and designed to withstand the demands of the job, so that you can minimize downtime and reduce maintenance costs.

In addition to the truck and equipment itself, it's also important to consider the support and maintenance services you'll need. This may include regular maintenance and repairs, as well as emergency support and replacement parts.

Finally, consider the reputation of the manufacturer and vendor when choosing your truck and equipment. Make sure to choose a reputable provider that has a proven track record of delivering quality equipment and support services.

In conclusion, choosing the right truck and equipment is a critical component of starting a successful dump truck business. By carefully evaluating your needs, budget, and options, and working with a reputable provider, you'll be well-positioned to choose the right equipment for your business and get the job done efficiently and effectively.

Chapter 9.   Hiring and Training Drivers and Staff

Hiring and training drivers and staff is a crucial component of starting a successful dump truck business. The right team can help you run your business efficiently and effectively, while the wrong team can result in increased costs, decreased productivity, and even safety hazards.

The first step in hiring and training drivers and staff is to assess your business needs. Consider the size of your business, the type of work you'll be doing, and the skills and experience you'll need from your drivers and staff. Based on this information, you can determine the number of drivers and staff you'll need and what roles they'll play in your business.

Once you've assessed your needs, it's important to carefully screen and interview potential employees. Make sure to verify their driving record, experience, and references, and assess their work ethic, communication skills, and compatibility with your business.

In addition to finding the right employees, it's also important to provide them with the right training. This may include training on the equipment they'll be using, as well as training on safety procedures, customer service, and other essential skills.

Another important factor to consider when hiring and training drivers and staff is compliance with state and federal regulations, such as those related to drug testing, background checks, and hours of service. Make sure to familiarize yourself with these regulations and ensure that your drivers and staff are in compliance.

In conclusion, hiring and training drivers and staff is a crucial component of starting a successful dump truck business. By carefully assessing your needs, screening and training employees, and staying compliant with regulations, you'll be well-positioned to build a strong and effective team that can help you grow your business and reach your goals.

Chapter 10.   Marketing and Advertising

Marketing and advertising are critical components of starting a successful dump truck business. The right marketing and advertising strategies can help you reach potential customers, establish your brand, and grow your business, while the wrong strategies can result in missed opportunities and decreased revenue.

The first step in developing a marketing and advertising strategy is to assess your target market. Consider the types of customers you want to reach, the services you'll offer, and the benefits you'll provide. Based on this information, you can develop a clear understanding of your target audience and what they're looking for in a dump truck business.

Once you've assessed your target market, it's important to develop a marketing plan that includes a mix of advertising and promotional activities. This may include developing a website and social media presence, creating promotional materials, and attending industry events and trade shows.

In addition to traditional advertising and marketing strategies, it's also important to consider word-of-mouth marketing and referral programs. Encourage satisfied customers to refer friends and family to your business, and offer incentives for doing so.

Another important factor to consider when developing a marketing and advertising strategy is your budget. Make sure to allocate enough resources to effectively market your business, while also being mindful of your overall expenses.

In conclusion, marketing and advertising are critical components of starting a successful dump truck business. By assessing your target market, developing a comprehensive marketing plan, and using a mix of traditional and innovative strategies, you'll be well-positioned to reach potential customers, establish your brand, and grow your business.

Chapter 11.   Establishing Strong Customer Relations

Establishing strong customer relationships is a key component of starting a successful dump truck business. Happy customers are more likely to use your services again and recommend you to others, while dissatisfied customers can harm your reputation and negatively impact your business.

The first step in establishing strong customer relationships is to understand your customers' needs and expectations. Ask for feedback, conduct surveys, and pay attention to the type of service your competitors are offering. Based on this information, you can tailor your services to meet the unique needs of your customers.

Another important factor to consider when establishing strong customer relationships is communication. Make sure to regularly communicate with your customers, and be responsive and proactive in addressing any concerns or issues they may have.

In addition to communication, it's also important to provide excellent customer service. Train your drivers and staff on the importance of customer service and how to effectively communicate with customers. Offer flexible and convenient services, and be willing to go above and beyond to meet your customers' needs.

Finally, consider offering incentives and rewards to your customers to encourage repeat business. This may include loyalty programs, discounts, and special promotions.

In conclusion, establishing strong customer relationships is a key component of starting a successful dump truck business. By understanding your customers' needs, providing excellent communication and customer service, and offering incentives and rewards, you'll be well-positioned to build strong and long-lasting relationships with your customers.

Chapter 12.   Establishing Rates and Billing Procedures

Establishing rates and billing procedures is an important part of starting a successful dump truck business. Your rates and billing procedures will directly impact your revenue, and it's important to get them right from the start.

The first step in establishing rates and billing procedures is to research the industry and determine the average rates for dump truck services in your area. This will give you a baseline to work from, and help you determine what rates are reasonable and competitive.

Once you've determined the average rates for your area, consider your own operating costs, including fuel, insurance, and maintenance costs. Make sure your rates cover these costs, while also allowing for a profit margin.

It's also important to consider the type of services you'll offer and the frequency with which you'll offer them. For example, will you offer one-time services or ongoing services? Will you charge a flat rate or an hourly rate?

In addition to establishing rates, it's also important to develop clear and transparent billing procedures. Make sure your customers understand what they're paying for and when they'll be billed. Consider offering multiple payment options, including online payment, to make it easy for customers to pay their bills.

Finally, make sure to regularly review your rates and billing procedures to ensure they're still competitive and aligned with your operating costs.

In conclusion, establishing rates and billing procedures is an important part of starting a successful dump truck business. By researching the industry, considering your operating costs, and developing clear and transparent billing procedures, you'll be well-positioned to establish rates and billing procedures that support your revenue goals.

Chapter 13. Maintaining a Safe and Efficient Fleet

Maintaining a safe and efficient fleet is crucial to the success of your dump truck business. Not only will this ensure the safety of your drivers and customers, but it will also help minimize downtime and reduce costs associated with maintenance and repairs.

The first step in maintaining a safe and efficient fleet is to regularly perform preventative maintenance on your trucks and equipment. This includes routine inspections, oil changes, and tire rotations, as well as more in-depth maintenance like engine rebuilds and transmission replacements.

It's also important to implement strict safety protocols for your drivers, including regular training and refresher courses. Make sure your drivers understand the importance of following traffic laws, properly securing loads, and conducting daily pre-trip inspections.

In addition to preventative maintenance and safety protocols, consider investing in technology to help improve the efficiency of your fleet. For example, GPS tracking systems can help you monitor your trucks' location, speed, and fuel consumption, allowing you to optimize routes and reduce costs.

Another important factor to consider when maintaining a safe and efficient fleet is compliance with regulatory requirements. Make sure your trucks and equipment meet all relevant federal and state regulations, and keep up-to-date with any changes or updates.

Finally, make sure to regularly evaluate the performance of your fleet and make any necessary adjustments to improve safety and efficiency.

In conclusion, maintaining a safe and efficient fleet is crucial to the success of your dump truck business. By regularly performing preventative maintenance, implementing strict safety protocols, investing in technology, and staying compliant with regulatory requirements, you'll be well-positioned to maintain a fleet that supports the growth and success of your business.

Chapter 14. Managing Operational Costs

Managing operational costs is a critical aspect of running a successful dump truck business. With the right strategies in place, you can minimize expenses, maximize profits, and stay competitive in a crowded market.

The first step in managing operational costs is to get a clear understanding of your expenses. This includes tracking fuel costs, maintenance and repair expenses, insurance costs, and payroll expenses. Once you have a good understanding of your costs, you can start identifying areas for improvement.

Fuel costs are one of the largest expenses for any trucking business, so it's important to find ways to reduce them. This may include optimizing routes to minimize fuel consumption, investing in more fuel-efficient trucks and equipment, and negotiating lower fuel prices with suppliers.

Maintenance and repair expenses can also be a significant cost, so it's important to have a preventative maintenance plan in place to minimize the need for repairs. This may include regularly scheduled maintenance, using high-quality parts and equipment, and ensuring your trucks are properly maintained and cleaned.

Insurance costs can also add up quickly, so it's important to compare rates and find the most cost-effective coverage. Consider working with an insurance broker to find the best coverage for your specific needs and budget.

Finally, payroll expenses can also take a significant portion of your budget, so it's important to carefully manage this expense as well. Consider offering competitive salaries and benefits, and finding ways to streamline payroll processes to minimize expenses.

In conclusion, managing operational costs is an essential aspect of running a successful dump truck business. By tracking expenses, identifying areas for improvement, and implementing cost-saving strategies, you can minimize expenses, maximize profits, and stay competitive in a crowded market.

Chapter 15.   Keeping Accurate Records and Bookkeeping

Keeping accurate records and bookkeeping are key components of running a successful dump truck business. Good record keeping not only helps you stay on top of your finances, but it also provides valuable insights into the health of your business, and helps you make informed decisions.

The first step in keeping accurate records is to establish a system for tracking your income and expenses. This may include using accounting software, manual bookkeeping, or a combination of both. Whatever system you choose, it's important to make sure it's easy to use, accurate, and up-to-date.

It's also important to keep track of all financial transactions, including invoices, receipts, and bank statements. This information can be used to track expenses, create financial reports, and prepare for tax season.

When it comes to bookkeeping, it's important to understand the basics of accounting and to keep accurate records of all financial transactions. This includes tracking income, expenses, and cash flow, as well as preparing financial statements such as balance sheets, income statements, and cash flow statements.

In addition to tracking financial transactions, it's also important to keep track of other important business information, such as contracts, licenses, and insurance policies. This information can be critical in the event of an audit or legal dispute, and should be stored in a secure, easily accessible location.

Finally, it's important to stay up-to-date with changes in tax laws and regulations, and to consult with a tax professional to ensure you're staying in compliance.

In conclusion, keeping accurate records and bookkeeping are essential components of running a successful dump truck business. By establishing a system for tracking your finances, keeping accurate records, and staying up-to-date with tax laws and regulations, you can stay on top of your finances and make informed decisions about the future of your business.

Chapter 16.   Staying Current with Industry Trends and Technological Advances

The dump truck industry is constantly evolving, with new technologies and innovations emerging all the time. To stay ahead of the competition and succeed in this rapidly-changing industry, it's essential to stay up-to-date with the latest trends and advancements.

One of the best ways to stay informed is by regularly attending industry events and conferences, where you can network with other dump truck business owners, learn about new technologies and best practices, and hear from experts in the field. You can also join industry associations and organizations, which often offer valuable resources and opportunities for professional development.

Another way to stay current is by staying informed about changes in regulations and safety standards, which can have a significant impact on your business. Make sure you're up-to-date with the latest requirements for things like truck maintenance, licensing, and insurance, and be prepared to adjust your business accordingly.

Investing in new technologies can also help you stay ahead of the curve. For example, you might consider investing in GPS tracking systems, automated dispatch software, or other technologies that can improve efficiency, streamline operations, and enhance customer service.

It's also important to stay on top of advances in the field of transportation and logistics. This includes keeping an eye on things like fuel efficiency, route optimization, and emerging technologies such as electric and autonomous vehicles. By staying informed about these developments, you can be better prepared to adapt to changes and take advantage of new opportunities as they arise.

In conclusion, staying current with industry trends and technological advances is crucial to the success of your dump truck business. By regularly attending industry events, staying informed about regulations and safety standards, investing in new technologies, and staying up-to-date with developments in the field of transportation and logistics, you can stay ahead of the competition and succeed in this rapidly-evolving industry.

Chapter 17.   Preparing for Emergencies and Contingencies

Running a dump truck business can be unpredictable at times, and unexpected events such as accidents, natural disasters, or equipment breakdowns can have a significant impact on your operations. To minimize the impact of these events, it's essential to have a plan in place for dealing with emergencies and contingencies.

One of the key things you can do to prepare for emergencies is to make sure that you have adequate insurance coverage for your business. This should include liability coverage for accidents, property damage coverage for your trucks and equipment, and insurance for lost income in the event of an interruption to your operations. Make sure you understand what your policy covers and what your responsibilities are in the event of a claim.

It's also important to have a plan in place for dealing with accidents and equipment breakdowns. This should include procedures for responding to emergencies, reporting accidents, and coordinating repairs. Make sure your drivers and other staff members are trained on these procedures and understand their role in responding to emergencies.

Another important aspect of preparing for emergencies is having contingency plans in place for dealing with disruptions to your operations. This might include having backup equipment on hand, working with other companies in your network to provide coverage in the event of an interruption, and having a plan in place for how you'll manage your business in the event of a natural disaster or other major event.

In conclusion, preparing for emergencies and contingencies is an essential part of running a successful dump truck business. By having adequate insurance coverage, a plan for responding to emergencies and equipment breakdowns, and contingency plans for dealing with disruptions to your operations, you can minimize the impact of unexpected events and keep your business running smoothly, even in difficult circumstances.

Chapter 18.   Staying on Top of Maintenance and Repairs

Keeping your fleet of dump trucks and equipment in top condition is essential for ensuring the efficiency and reliability of your operations. Regular maintenance and prompt repairs are key to preventing costly breakdowns and downtime, and to maintaining the safety of your drivers and equipment.

One of the most important things you can do to stay on top of maintenance and repairs is to develop a proactive maintenance schedule. This should include regular inspections of your trucks and equipment, routine maintenance tasks such as oil changes and tire rotations, and more extensive repairs as needed. Make sure you have a system in place for tracking when each piece of equipment is due for maintenance and for keeping records of all maintenance and repair work that's been done.

It's also important to establish a process for dealing with repairs as soon as they're needed. This might include having a team of in-house mechanics, or working with outside contractors who can provide repairs and maintenance services. Whatever approach you take, make sure you have the resources in place to respond quickly to any problems that arise.

Another important aspect of staying on top of maintenance and repairs is being proactive about identifying potential problems before they become major issues. This might include regularly inspecting your trucks and equipment for signs of wear and tear, monitoring their performance, and taking steps to address any issues that arise.

In conclusion, staying on top of maintenance and repairs is essential for ensuring the efficiency and reliability of your dump truck business. By developing a proactive maintenance schedule, having a process for dealing with repairs, and being proactive about identifying potential problems, you can keep your equipment in top condition and minimize the impact of downtime and repairs on your operations.

Chapter 19. Dealing with Insurance and Liability

As with any business, it's important to have the right insurance and liability coverage in place to protect your dump truck business from potential risks and liabilities. This will help you to manage the financial impact of any accidents, losses, or other incidents that may occur, and to ensure the continued success of your business.

There are several types of insurance that are important to consider when starting a dump truck business. These include liability insurance, which covers the costs of any damages or injuries that occur as a result of your business activities, and commercial vehicle insurance, which covers your trucks and other vehicles in the event of accidents, theft, or other losses.

It's important to thoroughly research your insurance options, and to work with a trusted insurance agent who understands the unique needs of your business. This will help you to find the right coverage for your needs, and to ensure that you're fully protected in the event of any incidents that may occur.

In addition to insurance, it's also important to consider your potential liability and the steps you can take to minimize this risk. This might include developing and implementing safety procedures and protocols, regularly training your drivers and staff, and taking steps to ensure that your trucks and equipment are well maintained and in good condition.

It's also important to stay informed about any changes to insurance laws and regulations, and to take steps to comply with any new requirements. This may involve seeking additional insurance coverage or updating your existing policies, and can

help you to avoid any legal or financial complications down the road.

Ultimately, by taking the time to properly manage your insurance and liability, you can give yourself peace of mind and ensure the long-term success of your dump truck business. This can help you to focus on growing your business and delivering top-notch services to your customers, and to avoid any unexpected costs or disruptions that could derail your progress.

So, make sure to invest in the right insurance and liability coverage, and to stay informed about any changes or developments in

this area. This will help you to protect your business and your assets, and to maintain a competitive advantage in the marketplace.

Additionally, consider seeking the advice of a legal professional who specializes in business insurance and liability. They can help you to understand the requirements and regulations specific to your industry and location, and to ensure that you're taking all the necessary steps to minimize your risks and liabilities.

Remember, protecting your dump truck business from potential risks and liabilities is a crucial part of your overall business strategy. By taking the necessary precautions and being proactive about your insurance and liability coverage, you can ensure the long-term success and stability of your business for years to come.

Chapter 20.   Preparing for Growth and Expansion

Growing your dump truck business can be an exciting and rewarding experience, but it also requires careful planning and preparation. By taking the time to consider your options and lay the foundation for growth, you can ensure a smooth and successful expansion process.

The first step in preparing for growth is to take a look at your current business operations. Evaluate your financials, your team, and your equipment to identify any areas that may need strengthening before you expand. This can help you to avoid any major disruptions or setbacks as you grow, and to ensure that you have the resources you need to succeed.

Next, consider your goals for growth. Do you want to expand your customer base, increase your profits, or enter new markets? Whatever your goals may be, make sure that they are clear and well-defined. This will help you to stay focused and motivated as you work towards expanding your business.

Another important factor to consider as you prepare for growth is your team. As your business grows, you may need to hire additional staff, or train and develop your current team to meet the demands of a larger operation. This can help you to ensure that your team is ready to take on the challenges of expansion, and to provide high-quality service to your customers.

Finally, be open to new opportunities and advancements in the industry. Stay informed about new technologies and trends in the dump truck business, and be willing to adapt and evolve as necessary. This can help you to stay ahead of the competition and to maintain a competitive advantage as you grow.

Preparing for growth and expansion can seem overwhelming, but with the right planning and preparation, you can successfully take your dump truck business to new heights. So, take the time to evaluate your current operations, set clear goals, build a strong team, and stay informed about industry developments, and you'll be well on your way to a successful expansion.

Chapter 21. Understanding the Hauling Process

Starting a dump truck business requires a deep understanding of the hauling process. This process is the backbone of your business and involves a series of steps that help you safely transport materials from one location to another. To make your dump truck business successful, you need to have a clear understanding of the hauling process and how to execute it efficiently.

The hauling process begins with the loading of materials onto the truck. It is crucial that the materials are loaded properly and securely so that they do not shift or fall during transit. This can be accomplished by using proper equipment and following industry standards for loading and securing materials.

Once the materials have been loaded, it's time to hit the road. It is important to follow the relevant laws and regulations while driving, such as speed limits, weight restrictions, and safety requirements. You also need to be mindful of road conditions and take necessary precautions to ensure the safety of your truck and the materials being transported.

Upon arrival at the destination, the unloading process begins. This involves safely removing the materials from the truck and delivering them to the appropriate location. It is important to follow industry standards for unloading materials to minimize the risk of injury or damage to property.

The hauling process is an important aspect of your dump truck business and it is essential that you understand it thoroughly. By following industry standards and best practices, you can ensure that your hauling process is efficient, safe, and successful.

Chapter 22.   Building Strong Relationships with Suppliers and Vendors

As a dump truck business owner, building strong relationships with suppliers and vendors is crucial to the success of your business. These relationships can provide you with access to quality materials and equipment, as well as helpful advice and support. By establishing strong relationships with suppliers and vendors, you can ensure that your business is well-equipped and well-supported, which can help you achieve your goals and succeed in the long term.

When building relationships with suppliers and vendors, it is important to focus on communication and trust. Establish clear lines of communication, and make sure to communicate regularly to keep each other informed about your needs and expectations. Additionally, it is important to be transparent and honest in all of your dealings, and to be fair and respectful in negotiations.

Another important aspect of building strong relationships with suppliers and vendors is to ensure that you are purchasing quality materials and equipment. It is important to do your research and choose suppliers and vendors that have a proven track record of providing high-quality products and services. Additionally, make sure to establish clear terms and conditions for your purchases, and be sure to pay on time to maintain good credit standing.

Finally, consider building long-term relationships with suppliers and vendors. This can be achieved by consistently meeting your obligations and delivering on your promises, as well as by offering incentives for good performance and addressing any issues or concerns in a prompt and professional manner. By building strong, long-term relationships with suppliers and vendors, you can ensure that your business has access to the resources it needs to succeed, and that you have a strong support system in place.

In conclusion, building strong relationships with suppliers and vendors is a key component of running a successful dump truck business. By focusing on communication, trust, quality, and long-term partnerships, you can establish relationships that will benefit your business for years to come.

Chapter 23. Streamlining Dispatch and Communication

Effective communication is the backbone of any successful business, and the dump truck industry is no exception. As you grow your business, it will become increasingly important to have a streamlined, efficient system in place for dispatching drivers and communicating with customers.

To get started, you'll need to assess your current communication system. This might mean looking at your existing dispatch software, or considering the use of new technologies such as GPS tracking, mobile apps, and real-time communication tools.

Once you've identified areas for improvement, it's time to start making changes. You may want to invest in new software or hardware, or train your staff on how to use existing tools more effectively. You may also want to establish clear protocols for communicating with drivers, customers, and suppliers.

Here are a few key steps you can take to streamline your dispatch and communication:

Invest in a reliable dispatch software that can help you manage your fleet, track drivers, and communicate with customers in real-time.

Establish clear protocols for communicating with drivers, including guidelines for responding to customer requests and updating schedules.

Make use of mobile communication tools, such as smartphones and tablets, to stay connected with drivers and customers on the go.

Train your staff on how to use dispatch software and other communication tools effectively.

Consider using GPS tracking and other advanced technologies to help you monitor your fleet in real-time, and to provide customers with up-to-date information on delivery times and progress.

By streamlining your dispatch and communication systems, you'll be able to respond quickly to customer requests and resolve any issues that arise. This will help you to maintain strong relationships with your customers, and to keep your business running smoothly.

Chapter 24. Implementing Fuel Management Strategies

Fuel is one of the biggest expenses for a dump truck business, and it's important to have a solid strategy in place to manage it. The goal is to reduce fuel costs and increase efficiency, which will help boost the bottom line. Here are some tips for managing fuel in your dump truck business:

Monitor fuel consumption: Keep track of how much fuel each truck is using and look for patterns or areas where you can improve efficiency.

Implement fuel-saving techniques: Encourage drivers to adopt fuel-saving techniques, such as accelerating and braking smoothly, keeping speeds at a steady rate, and avoiding idling whenever possible.

Choose fuel-efficient trucks: When buying new trucks, consider fuel efficiency as one of your priorities. Look for models with good fuel economy ratings, and keep in mind the weight of the load you'll be carrying.

Invest in fuel-saving technologies: Consider installing fuel-saving technologies, such as aerodynamic fairings, tire-pressure monitoring systems, and engine idle reduction systems. These can help reduce fuel consumption and improve your overall efficiency.

Shop around for fuel: Don't stick to just one fuel supplier. Shop around for the best prices and negotiate with suppliers to get a good deal.

Use fuel cards: Implement a fuel card system that allows drivers to purchase fuel at designated locations. This will help you track fuel expenses more effectively and eliminate the need for drivers to carry cash.

Conduct regular maintenance: Regular maintenance is essential to keeping your trucks running smoothly and efficiently. Make sure you stay on top of routine maintenance, such as oil changes, tune-ups, and tire rotations, to keep your trucks in good working order.

By following these tips and implementing fuel management strategies, you'll be able to keep your fuel costs under control, increase efficiency, and improve your bottom line.

Chapter 25.   Managing Fuel Costs

Fuel costs can quickly become one of the biggest expenses for your dump truck business, so it's important to stay on top of them. Here are some tips for managing fuel costs:

Shop Around for Fuel: Don't just buy fuel at the first station you come across. Take the time to research different fuel suppliers to find the best prices and deals.

Use Fuel Cards: Fuel cards allow you to track fuel purchases and monitor spending, making it easier to manage fuel costs. Plus, you may be able to get discounts or cash back rewards.

Implement Fuel-Efficient Driving Practices: Encourage your drivers to use fuel-efficient driving practices, such as accelerating gradually and keeping a steady speed. This can help to reduce fuel consumption and save money.

Monitor Fuel Usage: Keep an eye on fuel usage and track it regularly. This will help you to identify any areas where you may be able to reduce fuel costs.

Switch to Alternative Fuels: If diesel prices are high, consider switching to alternative fuels, such as biodiesel or compressed natural gas. This can help to reduce fuel costs and lower your carbon footprint.

Invest in Fuel-Efficient Equipment: Consider investing in fuel-efficient equipment, such as aerodynamic trucks and low-rolling-resistance tires. This can help to reduce fuel consumption and save money in the long run.

Stay Up-to-Date on Fuel Prices: Keep an eye on fuel prices and monitor any changes. This will help you to plan your fuel purchases and budget accordingly.

By following these tips, you can better manage fuel costs and keep your dump truck business running smoothly and efficiently.

Chapter 26.   Dealing with Environmental Concerns

As a dump truck business owner, you have a responsibility to take care of the environment and ensure that your operations don't cause any harm. The waste materials that you transport and dispose of can potentially pose a threat to the environment, so it's important to take steps to minimize the impact. Here are a few things to keep in mind.

Adhere to Regulations: The first and most important step is to make sure that you are fully compliant with all the local, state, and federal regulations regarding waste transportation and disposal. You must obtain all the necessary permits, licenses, and certifications required for your operations. This will help you avoid any penalties, fines, or legal action against your business.

Reduce Emissions: Your trucks will be on the road a lot, so it's essential to take measures to reduce emissions and minimize your carbon footprint. This includes regularly maintaining and servicing your vehicles, using fuel-efficient engines, and implementing eco-friendly driving practices.

Proper Disposal: When it comes to the waste materials you transport, you must ensure that they are disposed of properly. This means following all the guidelines and regulations regarding waste management, and avoiding any practices that could potentially harm the environment.

Green Initiatives: Show your customers and the community that you are committed to taking care of the environment by implementing green initiatives. For example, you could invest in recycling programs, use eco-friendly products, and promote sustainable practices in your workplace.

Educate Your Team: Make sure that your employees are aware of the importance of protecting the environment and are trained on the best practices for waste management and disposal. Encourage them to adopt eco-friendly habits and to be mindful of the impact of their actions.

By taking the steps outlined above, you can demonstrate your commitment to environmental responsibility and help build a positive reputation for your business. Plus, you'll be doing your part to ensure a cleaner and greener future for everyone.

Chapter 27.   Navigating the World of Permits and Licenses

Starting a dump truck business requires compliance with various permits and licenses, both at the local and federal levels. Failure to comply with the necessary permits and licenses can result in fines, legal trouble, and even the closure of your business. In this chapter, we'll explore the different types of permits and licenses you need to be aware of and how to obtain them.

First, you'll need to obtain a business license, which typically requires registering your business with the local government and paying a fee. You'll also need to obtain a tax identification number and register with your state's taxation department.

Second, you'll need to obtain a commercial driver's license (CDL) for each of your drivers. CDLs are mandatory for anyone operating commercial vehicles, such as dump trucks, and they require passing a written test and a skills test.

Third, you'll need to obtain a commercial vehicle registration for each of your dump trucks. This will typically require passing a vehicle inspection and paying a fee.

Fourth, you'll need to obtain permits for each of your dump trucks to operate on public roads. This may require obtaining a weight permit, an oversize/overweight permit, or a trip permit, depending on the size and weight of your dump truck and the materials it's hauling.

Finally, you'll need to comply with various environmental regulations, such as air and water pollution control laws, and waste disposal regulations. This may require obtaining permits from local and federal environmental agencies, as well as meeting certain standards for fuel consumption and emissions.

Overall, it's important to do your research and familiarize yourself with the permits and licenses required for your business. You may also want to consider consulting with a lawyer or a business advisor to ensure you have all your bases covered. By staying compliant with all necessary permits and licenses, you'll be able to operate your dump truck business without any legal issues.

Chapter 28.   Building a Strong Safety Culture

Starting a dump truck business comes with a lot of responsibility, and one of the most important aspects of that responsibility is keeping your drivers, customers, and the general public safe. That's why building a strong safety culture is so crucial to the success of your business.

Creating a safe work environment starts with having the right policies and procedures in place. This includes everything from proper truck maintenance and inspection to ensuring your drivers are trained on the best practices for operating their vehicles.

It's also important to establish a clear chain of command for safety-related issues. This means having a designated person responsible for overseeing safety, as well as clear procedures for reporting accidents or incidents.

In addition to having the right policies in place, it's essential to create a culture where safety is a priority. This means regularly communicating the importance of safety to your drivers and employees, and holding them accountable for following safety procedures.

One way to do this is by conducting regular safety meetings or training sessions to keep everyone informed of the latest industry trends and best practices. You can also use safety incentives, such as bonuses or rewards, to encourage safe behavior.

Another key aspect of building a strong safety culture is being proactive. This means anticipating potential safety risks and taking steps to prevent them before they become a problem. For example, you might conduct regular vehicle inspections to identify potential issues, or invest in new technologies, such as GPS tracking systems, to help monitor and improve driver behavior.

By making safety a top priority and building a culture that values it, you'll not only be doing the right thing for your employees and customers, but you'll also be protecting your business from costly accidents, insurance claims, and lawsuits.

Chapter 29. Staying Compliant with Federal and State Regulations

Starting a dump truck business can be a complex process, and one of the most critical aspects of success is staying compliant with all federal and state regulations. Failure to do so can result in hefty fines, legal issues, and damage to your reputation. Therefore, it's essential to understand the laws and regulations that apply to your business and make sure you are following them to the letter.

Federal Regulations

The Federal Motor Carrier Safety Administration (FMCSA) is the primary agency responsible for regulating the trucking industry in the United States. This agency sets standards for commercial truck drivers and carriers, such as minimum qualifications for drivers, hours of service restrictions, vehicle maintenance requirements, and more. It's crucial that you familiarize yourself with these regulations and make sure your business is following them.

State Regulations

In addition to federal regulations, each state has its set of laws and regulations that apply to the trucking industry. Some of the most common areas regulated by states include fuel taxes, insurance requirements, registration and licensing, and weight restrictions. It's essential that you research the regulations specific to your state and make sure your business is in compliance with them.

Insurance Requirements

Insurance is another critical aspect of compliance for dump truck businesses. The FMCSA requires all commercial truck carriers to have insurance coverage to protect themselves, their drivers, and the public. The minimum levels of insurance required by the FMCSA are $750,000 for liability insurance, $300,000 for uninsured/underinsured motorist coverage, and $100,000 for cargo insurance. You'll need to research the insurance requirements in your state and make sure your business is fully covered.

Stay Up-to-Date

It's essential to stay up-to-date with all federal and state regulations that apply to your business. Laws and regulations change frequently, and it's crucial that you keep up with these changes to make sure your business remains in compliance. You can stay informed by subscribing to industry newsletters, attending industry events, and consulting with legal and regulatory experts.

In conclusion, staying compliant with federal and state regulations is essential for the success of your dump truck business. By understanding and following the regulations, you'll protect your business from legal issues, fines, and damage to your reputation. Stay informed, stay up-to-date, and make compliance a top priority in your business.

Chapter 30.   Understanding the Importance of Insurance

Insurance is a critical component of any successful business, and starting a dump truck business is no exception. Not only does insurance protect you against financial losses and liability in the event of an accident or damage, but it also provides peace of mind and reassurance to your customers and employees. In this chapter, we'll delve into the different types of insurance you'll need for your dump truck business and why each is important.

Liability Insurance

Liability insurance is one of the most important types of insurance for a dump truck business. This type of insurance provides coverage in the event that you are held responsible for property damage or injury to someone else. For example, if one of your drivers causes an accident that damages a vehicle or injures another driver, your liability insurance will cover the costs of repairs or medical expenses. It's important to have adequate liability coverage in place to protect your business from potentially devastating financial losses.

Cargo Insurance

Cargo insurance is another critical type of insurance for a dump truck business. This insurance covers the cost of damages to the load you are transporting. For example, if your truck is involved in an accident and the load you are hauling is damaged or destroyed, your cargo insurance will cover the cost of replacing or repairing the load. This type of insurance is especially important if you are transporting expensive or fragile goods, as even a minor accident can result in significant losses.

Vehicle Insurance

Vehicle insurance is another important type of insurance for your dump truck business. This insurance covers the cost of repairs or replacement of your trucks in the event of an accident, theft, or damage. Whether you own one truck or a fleet, vehicle insurance is essential to protect your investment. It's also important to note that many states require commercial vehicles to have a certain level of insurance coverage.

Workers' Compensation Insurance

Finally, workers' compensation insurance is a critical type of insurance for any business that employs staff. This insurance covers the costs of medical expenses and lost wages for employees who are injured or become ill on the job. In the case of a dump truck business, workers' compensation insurance is particularly important given the potential for on-the-job accidents or injuries.

In conclusion, insurance is a critical component of a successful dump truck business. By investing in liability insurance, cargo insurance, vehicle insurance, and workers' compensation insurance, you can protect your business from financial losses and ensure that your employees and customers are covered in the event of an accident or injury.

Chapter 31. Navigating the World of Taxation

Starting a dump truck business can be a rewarding experience, but it also comes with its share of challenges, including the often-complex world of taxation. With so many different types of taxes to keep track of and regulations to follow, it's essential to have a solid understanding of the tax landscape.

First and foremost, it's important to determine what type of business structure your dump truck business will take, as this will affect the types of taxes you'll be required to pay. Will you be operating as a sole proprietorship, partnership, limited liability company (LLC), or corporation? Each structure has its own set of tax implications, so it's essential to consult with a tax professional to determine the best option for your business.

Once you have determined your business structure, it's time to start thinking about the different types of taxes you'll need to pay. These can include income taxes, self-employment taxes, sales taxes, and fuel taxes, among others. It's important to stay up-to-date on all the latest tax laws and regulations, as these can change from year to year.

Another important aspect of taxation is record-keeping. Keeping accurate and up-to-date records of all your business transactions will make it easier to file your taxes and ensure you're paying the correct amount. This can include things like receipts, invoices, and other financial documents.

Finally, it's important to remember that the tax landscape is constantly changing, so it's essential to stay informed and work with a knowledgeable tax professional who can help you navigate the complexities of the tax system. Whether you're just starting out or are looking to grow your business, having a strong understanding of the tax landscape is critical to your success.

In conclusion, while taxation can be a complex and overwhelming aspect of starting a dump truck business, it's an essential part of the process. By taking the time to understand the tax landscape and working with a knowledgeable professional, you can ensure that your business is compliant with all relevant regulations and that you're paying the correct amount of taxes.

Chapter 32.   Building a Strong Employee Benefits Program

Starting a dump truck business requires hard work and dedication, but it also requires a team of skilled and motivated employees. Your team is the backbone of your business, and it's important to invest in their well-being. One way to do this is by building a strong employee benefits program.

A comprehensive benefits program can help you attract and retain top talent, increase employee satisfaction and loyalty, and boost productivity. It can also set your business apart from competitors and enhance your reputation as a responsible employer.

But with so many options to choose from, it can be overwhelming to determine the best benefits for your business. Here are some key components to consider when developing your employee benefits program:

Health Insurance: Providing health insurance is a crucial part of any benefits program. It helps employees stay healthy, reduces absenteeism, and increases job satisfaction. Consider offering a range of health insurance options, such as HMOs, PPOs, and high-deductible plans.

Retirement Benefits: Offering a retirement savings plan, such as a 401(k) or an IRA, can help employees prepare for their future and increase their overall financial security. Consider matching a portion of their contributions to encourage participation.

Paid Time Off (PTO): Allowing employees to take paid time off for holidays, vacation, and personal days is an important way to support work-life balance and increase job satisfaction. Consider offering a flexible PTO policy that allows employees to take the time they need when they need it.

Training and Development: Investing in employee training and development can increase employee satisfaction and boost their skills and knowledge. Consider offering on-the-job training, workshops, and online courses to help employees grow and develop professionally.

Employee Assistance Programs (EAPs): EAPs provide a range of services, such as counseling and financial planning, to help employees manage stress, mental health, and personal problems. EAPs can improve employee well-being and productivity.

Flexible Work Arrangements: Offering flexible work arrangements, such as telecommuting or flexible schedules, can help employees balance their work and personal lives and increase job satisfaction.

Employee Discounts: Offering discounts on products and services can help employees save money and increase their overall job satisfaction.

By offering a comprehensive benefits program, you can create a positive work environment and support the well-being of your employees. This can increase their productivity, reduce turnover, and help your business thrive.

Chapter 33. Maintaining Strong Relationships with Customers

Starting and running a successful dump truck business takes a lot of hard work and dedication. But, what really sets a great business apart from the rest is the relationships it builds with its customers. No matter how great your trucks and equipment are, or how skilled your drivers are, you won't get very far without satisfied customers.

Building strong relationships with customers is all about communication, reliability, and trust. Let's take a look at each of these key components in more detail.

Communication: Communication is key when it comes to building strong relationships with customers. You want to be responsive and proactive when it comes to addressing their needs and concerns. This means being available when they need you and being proactive in offering solutions when problems arise. Regular check-ins with customers can also help to keep the lines of communication open and ensure that everyone is on the same page.

Reliability: Customers want to know that they can count on you to get the job done, and done well. This means meeting deadlines, being on time, and delivering on your promises. When customers see that you're reliable, they'll be more likely to trust you and continue doing business with you.

Trust: Trust is the foundation of any strong relationship. When customers trust you, they know that you'll always be there for them and that you have their best interests at heart. This trust takes time to build, but it can be done by consistently delivering high-quality service, being transparent in your dealings with them, and following through on your commitments.

In order to maintain strong relationships with customers, it's also important to be flexible and responsive to their needs. This means being open to their suggestions and feedback, and making changes when necessary to better meet their needs. A willingness to go above and beyond for your customers can also help to solidify your relationship with them.

Finally, it's also important to reward loyal customers. This could mean offering special promotions, discounts, or other incentives to show them that you value their business. Regular follow-ups and check-ins can also help to keep the relationship strong and ensure that customers feel appreciated.

Building and maintaining strong relationships with customers takes time, effort, and dedication. But, by focusing on communication, reliability, and trust, you can create a business that not only provides quality services, but also forms strong bonds with its customers. And, when you have happy customers, you'll have a successful business.

Chapter 34.   Establishing a Strong Reputation in the Industry

Starting and growing a trucking business is a challenging but rewarding experience. It requires a lot of hard work, dedication, and perseverance. One of the most critical elements to the success of your business is building a strong reputation in the industry. When you have a strong reputation, it's easier to attract new customers, retain existing ones, and grow your business.

Here are some key strategies for establishing a strong reputation in the trucking industry:

Provide excellent customer service The foundation of a strong reputation is providing excellent customer service. Make sure that your drivers are trained in effective communication and problem-solving techniques. Respond to customer inquiries and complaints promptly, and do everything you can to resolve any issues to their satisfaction.

Offer high-quality services Offer high-quality services that meet or exceed customer expectations. Make sure your trucks and equipment are well-maintained and reliable. Ensure that your drivers are knowledgeable, professional, and respectful. Continuously strive to improve the quality of your services to ensure customer satisfaction.

Adhere to industry regulations and standards Stay up-to-date with industry regulations and standards, and make sure your business is fully compliant. This shows that you are a responsible and trustworthy business that operates with integrity.

Build strong relationships with suppliers and vendors Strong relationships with suppliers and vendors can help build your reputation and lead to more business opportunities. Work with them to ensure a smooth and efficient supply chain that benefits everyone.

Foster a positive work environment Create a positive work environment for your employees. When your employees are happy and motivated, they are more likely to provide excellent customer service and to take pride in their work.

Participate in industry events and organizations Participate in industry events and organizations, such as trade shows and professional associations. This helps to keep you informed about the latest industry trends and news, and gives you the opportunity to network and build relationships with other industry professionals.

Leverage social media and online reviews Social media and online reviews can play a significant role in building your reputation. Encourage satisfied customers to leave positive reviews and respond to any negative feedback constructively.

In conclusion, building a strong reputation in the trucking industry requires a combination of providing excellent customer service, offering high-quality services, adhering to industry regulations, building strong relationships, fostering a positive work environment, participating in industry events and organizations, leveraging social media, and online reviews.

Chapter 35.   Making the Most of Technology and Automation

Technology and automation play a crucial role in the success of any modern business, and the transportation industry is no exception. From communication to dispatch and beyond, technology can streamline operations, reduce costs, and improve efficiency. Here's what you need to know to make the most of technology and automation in your transportation business.

Start with a Solid IT Foundation

Before you dive into the world of technology, it's important to make sure you have a solid IT foundation in place. This includes reliable hardware, software, and network systems, as well as a team of IT professionals who can help you get the most out of your technology investments.

Invest in Communication and Dispatch Technology

When it comes to transportation, effective communication and dispatch are key. This is where technology can really shine. Invest in a dispatch and communication system that integrates seamlessly with your existing systems and processes. Look for features like GPS tracking, real-time delivery updates, and mobile capabilities to help you stay connected with your drivers and customers at all times.

Streamline Your Operations with Automation

From route planning and optimization to invoicing and record-keeping, there are many aspects of your transportation business that can be automated. This not only helps you save time and reduce errors, but it also allows you to focus on more strategic initiatives. Look for automation tools that can help you streamline your operations, such as route optimization software, electronic invoicing systems, and fleet management software.

Maximize Efficiency with Data and Analytics

Data and analytics play a crucial role in helping you make informed decisions and stay ahead of the competition. From tracking fuel consumption and maintenance costs to monitoring driver performance, there is a wealth of information that can be used to improve your operations. Look for tools that can help you collect and analyze this data, and use the insights you gain to drive continuous improvement.

Stay Ahead of the Curve

Technology and automation are rapidly evolving, so it's important to stay ahead of the curve. Keep an eye on industry trends and new technologies, and be prepared to adapt and adopt new solutions as they emerge. By doing so, you'll be well-positioned to stay competitive and continue to grow your business.

In conclusion, technology and automation are powerful tools that can help you streamline your operations, reduce costs, and improve efficiency. By investing in the right solutions, you can take your transportation business to the next level and stay ahead of the competition. So why wait? Start exploring the world of technology and automation today!

Chapter 36. Building Strong Relationships with Local Communities

As a trucking business, you are an important member of the local community. Building strong relationships with the community is crucial to your success, as well as to the health and well-being of the community as a whole. Here are some tips for building and maintaining strong relationships with your local community:

Get involved in local events and activities. Attend local events, such as festivals, parades, and charity walks. Offer to sponsor local sports teams, or volunteer at local schools or community centers. These events are a great opportunity to get to know the community, and show that you are an active and supportive member of the community.

Participate in local organizations and committees. Join local organizations, such as Chamber of Commerce or Rotary Club, and actively participate in meetings and events. This allows you to network with other local businesses, and show your commitment to the community.

Support local charities and organizations. Choose a local charity or organization that is important to you and your business, and support it through donations or volunteer work. This not only helps the community, but also shows that your business is a good corporate citizen.

Be responsive to the community's needs. Pay attention to what the community needs, and try to meet those needs in a responsible and responsive manner. This could mean anything from participating in a neighborhood cleanup effort, to offering to donate goods or services in times of need.

Be open and transparent. Keep the community informed about your business activities, and be willing to address any concerns they may have. Hold regular town hall meetings or open houses, and respond promptly to questions or complaints. This helps build trust and credibility with the community.

Practice environmental responsibility. Be mindful of your impact on the environment, and take steps to minimize any negative effects. This could mean investing in fuel-efficient vehicles, reducing emissions, or taking steps to reduce waste.

Building strong relationships with your local community is essential to the success of your trucking business. By being an active and supportive member of the community, and by being responsive to their needs, you can build a strong reputation and help ensure the long-term health and well-being of your community.

Chapter 37.   Understanding the Importance of Environmental Stewardship

As a business owner in the transportation industry, you have a responsibility to be a good steward of the environment. Not only is this important for the health and well-being of the planet and its inhabitants, but it can also impact the success and growth of your business.

To begin, it's important to understand the different ways that your business can impact the environment. This might include emissions from vehicles, fuel consumption, waste generated through daily operations, and more.

Once you understand the areas where you can make a difference, it's time to start taking action. Here are a few steps you can take to build a culture of environmental stewardship within your organization:

Set environmental goals and track your progress. Establishing specific, measurable goals can help you stay on track as you work towards a more sustainable future. Track your progress regularly and celebrate your successes along the way.

Invest in eco-friendly technologies and practices. Whether it's transitioning to a more fuel-efficient fleet, implementing recycling programs, or using more sustainable cleaning products, investing in environmentally-friendly practices can have a big impact.

Train employees on the importance of environmental stewardship. Your employees are the front line of your business, so it's essential to educate them on the importance of reducing your impact on the environment. Encourage them to adopt environmentally-friendly habits both on and off the job.

Partner with other businesses and organizations to promote environmental stewardship. Collaborating with like-minded organizations can help you achieve your goals more quickly and effectively. Look for opportunities to work with suppliers, vendors, and other businesses to make a difference in your community.

Engage with your customers and communities on environmental issues. Your customers and communities care about the environment, and they want to know what you're doing to make a positive impact. Share your progress and successes with them, and encourage them to get involved in your efforts.

By taking these steps, you can establish a strong culture of environmental stewardship within your organization. This will not only help you minimize your impact on the environment, but it can also help you build a positive reputation in your industry and community.

In conclusion, environmental stewardship is an important responsibility for all businesses, and the transportation industry is no exception. By taking steps to reduce your impact on the environment, you can not only do your part to protect the planet, but you can also improve the success and growth of your business.

Chapter 38. Staying Up-to-Date with Industry Best Practices

Running a successful trucking company is a big job, and it's important to stay informed about the latest industry best practices to stay ahead of the competition and provide the best possible service to your customers. Whether it's new regulations, technological advancements, or changes in customer preferences, staying up-to-date is essential for success in the trucking industry.

One way to stay informed is to attend trade shows and conferences. These events bring together industry leaders, experts, and fellow trucking professionals to share their knowledge and experience. They also provide opportunities to network and make valuable connections with others in the industry.

Another way to stay informed is by reading industry publications and trade journals. These sources provide valuable insights into industry trends, advancements, and challenges, and can help you stay ahead of the curve.

It's also important to stay up-to-date with regulations and laws. The trucking industry is heavily regulated, and failing to comply with regulations can result in hefty fines and damage to your company's reputation. Stay informed about changes in regulations and make sure that your company is in compliance at all times.

Investing in technology is another way to stay ahead of the curve. Automation and digital solutions can help streamline processes, improve efficiency, and increase productivity. They can also help you provide better service to your customers and reduce costs.

Finally, building strong relationships with suppliers and vendors is crucial. These partners can provide valuable insights and advice on industry trends and best practices, as well as help you stay up-to-date on the latest technology and solutions.

In conclusion, staying up-to-date with industry best practices is essential for success in the trucking industry. Attend trade shows and conferences, read industry publications and trade journals, stay informed about regulations, invest in technology, and build strong relationships with suppliers and vendors to stay ahead of the curve.

Chapter 39. Navigating the World of Fleet Management

As a trucking company, having a well-managed fleet is crucial to your success. Fleet management involves a variety of tasks and responsibilities, including maintaining the safety and efficiency of your vehicles, making the most of technology and automation, and staying up-to-date with industry best practices. In this chapter, we will dive into the world of fleet management and explore some of the key elements that are essential for success.

Maintaining a Safe and Efficient Fleet One of the most important aspects of fleet management is ensuring the safety and efficiency of your vehicles. This includes regularly performing maintenance and repairs, staying compliant with federal and state regulations, and building a strong safety culture. It's also important to stay on top of maintenance and repairs, as well as to prepare for emergencies and contingencies.

Making the Most of Technology and Automation Technology and automation can be powerful tools in the world of fleet management. For example, using GPS tracking systems and dispatch software can help you keep track of your vehicles and streamline communication with drivers. Additionally, implementing fuel management strategies and monitoring fuel costs can help you save money and improve the overall efficiency of your fleet.

Staying Up-to-Date with Industry Best Practices The trucking industry is constantly evolving, and it's essential to stay up-to-date with the latest best practices and trends. This includes keeping an eye on emerging technologies, attending industry events and conferences, and networking with other trucking professionals. Additionally, staying current with industry trends and technological advances can help you identify new opportunities for growth and expansion.

Building Strong Relationships with Suppliers and Vendors Building strong relationships with suppliers and vendors is also crucial for success in the world of fleet management. This includes working with trusted mechanics and maintenance providers, as well as building strong relationships with fuel and tire suppliers. By cultivating these relationships, you can ensure that you have access to the resources you need to keep your fleet running smoothly and efficiently.

Navigating the World of Permits and Licenses Finally, it's important to understand the complex world of permits and licenses in the trucking industry. This includes staying compliant with federal and state regulations, as well as navigating the permit and licensing process for your vehicles and drivers. With the right resources and support, you can ensure that your trucking business stays on the right side of the law and avoids any costly legal or regulatory problems.

In conclusion, fleet management is a complex and challenging field, but by following best practices, making the most of technology and automation, and building strong relationships with suppliers and vendors, you can ensure the success and growth of your trucking business. Whether you're just starting out or are a seasoned pro, there is always more to learn and opportunities to explore in the world of fleet management.

Chapter 40. Preparing for the Future of the Dump Truck Business

As a business owner in the dump truck industry, it's important to always be thinking ahead and preparing for what the future may bring. The world of business is constantly evolving and it's essential to stay ahead of the curve to ensure the longevity and success of your company. In this chapter, we'll explore some key strategies for preparing for the future of the dump truck business.

Stay on Top of Industry Trends: The dump truck industry is constantly changing and it's important to stay up-to-date with the latest trends and advancements. Read industry publications, attend conferences, and network with other business owners to stay in the know. This will give you a competitive advantage and help you stay ahead of the curve.

Invest in Technology: Technology is playing an increasingly important role in the dump truck industry and it's crucial to invest in the right tools to stay ahead of the competition. From GPS tracking systems to automated dispatch and billing systems, there are many technologies available to help streamline your operations and increase efficiency.

Diversify Your Services: Diversifying your services can help you tap into new markets and increase your revenue streams. Consider offering additional services such as demolition, site preparation, or excavation to expand your customer base.

Build Strong Relationships with Suppliers and Vendors: Building strong relationships with your suppliers and vendors is crucial for the success of your business. Maintaining good communication and ensuring that you are getting the best prices on the products and services you need will help you keep your costs down and improve your bottom line.

Foster a Positive Work Environment: A positive work environment is key to attracting and retaining the best employees. By creating a culture of teamwork, respect, and open communication, you can build a strong and motivated workforce that is dedicated to the success of your business.

Plan for the Future: Finally, it's important to have a clear vision and plan for the future of your business. Set achievable goals, create a budget, and make a plan for how you will reach those goals. This will give you a roadmap for success and help you navigate the ups and downs of the business world.

By staying on top of industry trends, investing in technology, diversifying your services, building strong relationships with suppliers and vendors, fostering a positive work environment, and planning for the future, you can set your dump truck business up for success in the years to come. Remember, the key to success in any business is preparation and a willingness to adapt to change. So be proactive, stay focused, and never stop learning, and you'll be well on your way to success in the dump truck industry.

here are a few tips for success in the dump truck business:

Always put the customer first: Happy customers lead to repeat business and positive word-of-mouth recommendations.

Stay organized and keep accurate records: This will help you stay on top of finances, maintenance, and regulations.

Invest in technology and automation: This can help streamline processes, reduce costs, and increase efficiency.

Maintain a well-trained and motivated workforce: Your employees are the backbone of your business, and their satisfaction and performance will impact your success.

Stay up-to-date with industry trends and best practices: This will help you stay competitive and make informed business decisions.

Build strong relationships with suppliers, vendors, and the local community: These relationships will help you secure the resources you need to grow and succeed.

Continuously evaluate and improve processes: This will help you identify areas for improvement and ensure that your business remains efficient and profitable.

With these tips and a commitment to excellence, we wish you all the best as you navigate the world of the dump truck business. Good luck, and we hope that your business thrives!

As you come to the end of this book, we hope you have gained a better understanding of the world of dump truck business and all the elements that go into running a successful operation. From hiring and training drivers and staff, to managing operational costs and staying on top of maintenance and repairs, there are many different aspects to consider.

But with hard work and dedication, there is no reason why you can't build a thriving and profitable dump truck business that stands the test of time. Whether you're just starting out or you're looking to expand an existing operation, remember to stay focused on your goals, stay up-to-date with industry best practices, and build strong relationships with customers, suppliers, and local communities.

We wish you all the best in your journey and success in your dump truck business. Remember to always keep pushing forward and never give up on your dreams. Good luck!

www.ingramcontent.com/pod-product-compliance
Lightning Source LLC
Chambersburg PA
CBHW071055290526
45795CB00004B/1507